CRAFTY Badges

Petra Boase

Gareth Stevens Publishing
A WORLD ALMANAC EDUCATION GROUP COMPANY

The original publishers would like to thank the following children for modeling for this book: Danny Bill, Emma Currie, Vicky Dummigan, Kirsty Fraser, Cherine Henry, Barry Lee, Kirsty Lee, Mickey Malku, Sharday Manahan, Nancy Miller, and Letitia Williams. Thanks also to their parents and Walnut Tree Walk Primary School.

For a free color catalog describing Gareth Stevens' list of high-quality books and multimedia programs, call 1-800-542-2595 (USA) or 1-800-461-9120 (Canada). Gareth Stevens Publishing's Fax: (414) 225-0377.

Library of Congress Cataloging-in-Publication Data

Boase, Petra.
    Crafty badges / by Petra Boase.
        p. cm. — (Crafty kids)
    Includes bibliographical references and index.
    Summary: Provides instructions for creating all kinds of decorative pins from cardboard, papier-mâché, felt, wood, salt dough, and other easily obtainable materials.
    ISBN 0-8368-2500-4 (lib. bdg.)
    1. Handicraft—Juvenile literature. 2. Badges—Juvenile literature. 3. Salt dough craft—Juvenile literature. 4. Papier-mâché—Juvenile literature. [1. Handicraft. 2. Jewelry making.] I. Title. II. Series.
TT160.B63   2000
745.5—dc21   99-42735

This North American edition first published in 2000 by
Gareth Stevens Publishing
A World Almanac Education Group Company
1555 North RiverCenter Drive, Suite 201
Milwaukee, WI 53212 USA

Original edition © 1996 by Anness Publishing Limited. First published in 1996 by Lorenz Books, an imprint of Anness Publishing Limited, New York, New York. This U.S. edition © 2000 by Gareth Stevens, Inc. Additional end matter © 2000 by Gareth Stevens, Inc.

Senior editor: Sue Grabham
Assistant editor: Sophie Warne
Photographer: John Freeman
Designer: Michael R. Carter
Gareth Stevens series editor: Dorothy L. Gibbs
Editorial assistant: Diane Laska-Swanke

Printed in Mexico

1 2 3 4 5 6 7 8 9 04 03 02 01 00

Introduction

Badges are a lot of fun to wear and not very expensive to make. Many of the materials for making badges, such as cereal boxes, candy wrappers, and scraps of fabric, can be found around the house.

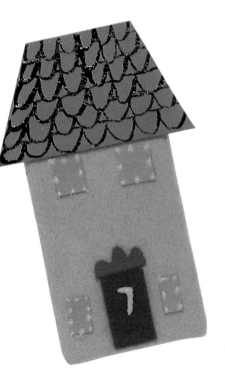

Before making badges, prepare your work area. Use newspaper to cover the work surface, so you will not damage it, and organize all the materials you need ahead of time. If you have questions or need help, ask an adult. After you make a badge, be sure the badge pin is attached securely, or the badge might fall off when you wear it.

Besides wearing badges on shirts and other clothing, you can jazz up hats and bags with them. Badges also make great gifts for family and friends. Just follow the instructions in this book to make your masterpieces!

Petra Boase

Contents

GETTING STARTED

BADGE FUN

Materials

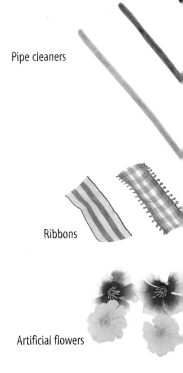

ACRYLIC PAINTS
Because there are so many different kinds of paints, it is important to read the instructions on the tube or bottle to make sure that particular paint is suitable for your project.

ARTIFICIAL FLOWERS
Flowers made of plastic or fabric can be cut off at the stem and glued onto a badge.

BUTTONS
Look for old buttons in all shapes, sizes, and colors around the house or in secondhand stores. New buttons can be purchased at stores that sell sewing supplies or craft materials.

COTTON
A roll of cotton can be purchased at a drug store. Cotton is easily glued onto cardboard to make badges such as "Fluffy Snowman."

CREPE PAPER
This strong, slightly stretchy paper comes in many bright colors. It is good for making paper flowers.

FABRIC PAINTS
These special paints are made for decorating fabric. Be sure to let the paint dry completely before touching it.

FAKE FUR
Pieces of fuzzy material that look and feel like fur are available at craft stores in a variety of colors. This material can be cut and glued.

FELT
This fabric is easy to cut, and it does not fray. When gluing it onto cardboard, use only a small amount of glue.

FIMO
This claylike, plastic modeling compound comes in a range of bright colors, and it becomes hard and durable when it is baked. Because it is a plastic material, it can be somewhat more difficult to handle than natural clay. Be sure to read the instructions on the package carefully before using it.

GRASS PAPER
This paper looks like grass. You can buy it at stores that sell craft supplies. If it is not available, green felt can be used instead.

PIPE CLEANERS
These pieces of fuzzy covered wire come in an assortment of colors and sizes and can be coiled and bent to make fun shapes. You will need strong glue to attach them to a badge.

Pipe cleaners

Ribbons

Artificial flowers

Buttons

RIBBONS
These strips of fabric come in many different colors and widths. They can be used to make bows for badges such as "Birthday Present."

GLITTER
Loose glitter can be sprinkled onto glue to decorate badges.

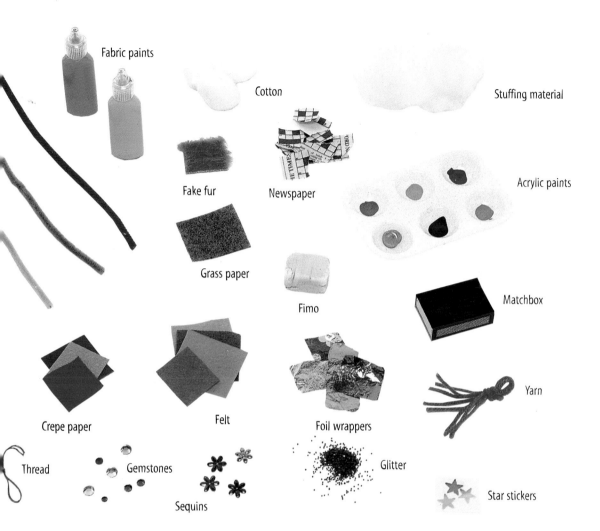

Fabric paints

Cotton

Stuffing material

Fake fur

Newspaper

Acrylic paints

Grass paper

Fimo

Matchbox

Crepe paper

Felt

Foil wrappers

Yarn

Thread

Gemstones

Glitter

Sequins

Star stickers

GEMSTONES
These imitation gems are usually made of plastic and are used for decoration. They are available at stores that sell art and craft supplies.

SEQUINS
Glue these jewel-like decorations onto the surface of a badge to add sparkle.

FOIL WRAPPERS
Save the foil wrappers from candy bars. They can be smoothed out and used to cover your badge shapes.

STAR STICKERS
These shiny, star-shaped pieces of paper have an adhesive backing and come in all sorts of colors.

NEWSPAPER
Use newspaper, torn into small pieces, to make papier-mâché. Also use newspaper to protect your work surface.

STUFFING MATERIAL
Several kinds of stuffing material, including scrunched-up paper, can be used to fill fabric shapes.

Equipment

CARDBOARD

You will need cardboard of thin to medium thickness to make badge shapes. The thin cardboard from empty cereal boxes works well.

RULER

You will need a ruler to measure cardboard, fabric, and other materials and to draw straight lines.

PAPER FASTENERS

These small brass fasteners can be used to hold pieces of paper or cardboard together.

WHITE GLUE AND GLUE BRUSH

Undiluted, white glue is used to hold materials together. Diluted with water, it can be used to make papier-mâché.

PAINTBRUSH

You will need at least one paintbrush, but you might want to have several in different sizes and thicknesses. Remember to wash paintbrushes thoroughly after using them.

MASKING TAPE

Although not as strong as electrical tape, masking tape is useful for holding materials together temporarily.

ELECTRICAL TAPE

This strong tape comes in a variety of colors and is very useful for attaching pins securely to the backs of badges. Colored electrical tape is also good for decorating badges.

COMPASS

Use a compass to draw perfect circles. If you do not have a compass, you can draw around a cup or a drinking glass. You can use the sharp point of a compass to poke small holes, but be very careful, or ask an adult to help.

COOKIE CUTTERS

Use cookie cutters of various shapes to cut badge designs out of salt dough. Remember to clean the cookie cutters thoroughly after using them.

MODELING TOOL

This special tool is used for cutting and shaping clay, salt dough, or Fimo.

ROLLING PIN

You will need this kitchen tool to roll out salt dough, Fimo, and other modeling materials.

SANDPAPER

You will need a fine grade of sandpaper to smooth out the surfaces and the edges of salt dough badges.

Masking tape

Electrical tape

Scissors

SCISSORS

The blades and points of scissors can be very sharp, so be careful when using them to cut paper, thin cardboard, and fabric. Always sit down when using scissors, and keep the tips pointed away from your body.

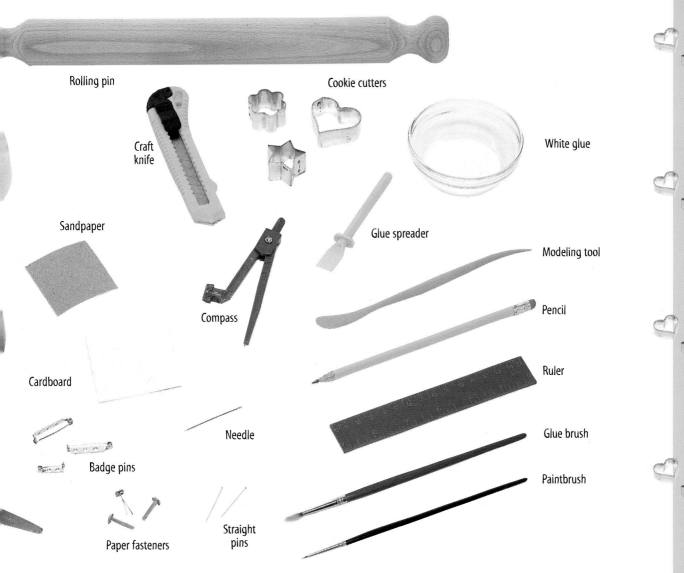

Rolling pin

Cookie cutters

White glue

Craft knife

Glue spreader

Modeling tool

Sandpaper

Pencil

Compass

Cardboard

Ruler

Needle

Glue brush

Badge pins

Paintbrush

Paper fasteners

Straight pins

BADGE PINS

These special pins have a flat side that can be glued to the back of a badge. They are found in various sizes at most craft shops and art supply stores. If badge pins are not available, you can use safety pins.

NEEDLE AND STRAIGHT PINS

You will need a needle and straight pins for badges that require sewing. Be careful! They have sharp points. Use straight pins to hold pieces of fabric together while you sew them.

CRAFT KNIFE

This special kind of knife has a razor-sharp edge that can cut through thick materials. Because it is an extremely dangerous tool, always have an adult do the cutting for you.

How to Make Salt Dough

YOU WILL NEED

- 2 ½ cups (350 grams) flour
- 1 cup (280 g) salt
- ¾ cup (180 milliliters) water
- 2 tablespoons (30 ml) vegetable oil

1 Measure out all ingredients. Put the flour and the salt into a bowl and mix well.

2 Continue mixing as you gradually pour the water over the salt and flour.

3 Pour in the vegetable oil and mix well.

4 Place the salt dough on a clean surface that has been dusted with flour. Knead the dough until it is firm, then put it in an airtight container or wrap it in plastic wrap. Put the dough in the refrigerator for half an hour before using it.

How to Make Papier-Mâché

YOU WILL NEED
- Newspaper
- White glue
- Water

1 Tear sheets of newspaper into small pieces. Make a runny paste with white glue and water by adding water to the glue, a little at a time.

2 Dip pieces of newspaper into the runny paste. Coat each piece completely, then stick it onto a cardboard shape. Apply three or four layers of newspaper this way. Let the papier-mâché dry overnight in a warm, dry place.

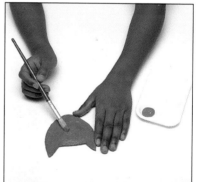

3 Paint the papier-mâché. When the paint is completely dry, apply a layer of varnish to protect it. Use either a water-based varnish or a mixture of white glue and water.

Making a Template

1 Cover the template pattern with a sheet of tracing paper. Use masking tape to hold the tracing paper in place. Trace over the outline of the pattern with a pencil.

2 Remove the tracing paper from the template pattern. Turn the paper over and, on the back side of the tracing paper, rub over the traced outline with a pencil.

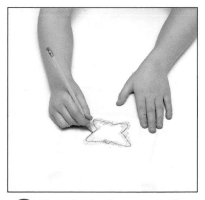

3 Place the tracing paper, with the rubbed side facedown, on a piece of cardboard. Draw over the outline with a pencil to transfer the pattern onto the cardboard.

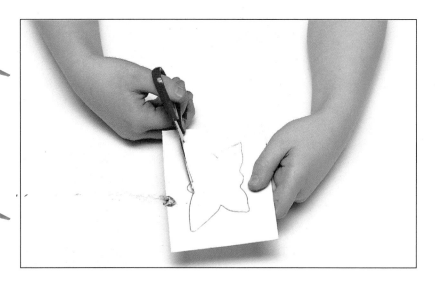

4 To make the template, remove the tracing paper and cut out the cardboard shape. To use the template, place it on the material from which you will make the badge and draw around it with a pencil or a marker. Save the template to use again.

Feather template pattern for "Feathery Chicken" badge on pages 18-19

Chicken template pattern for "Feathery Chicken" badge on pages 18-19

Dog template pattern for "Felt Scotty Dog" badge on pages 28-29

13

Papier-Mâché Cat

Watch this cat's eyes twinkle under bright lights. The gemstones used for the eyes can be purchased at most art supply stores and craft shops.

YOU WILL NEED
- Pencil
- Cardboard
- Scissors
- Newspaper
- White glue and glue brush
- Water
- Acrylic paints
- Paintbrush
- Varnish
- Felt
- Gemstones
- Pipe cleaners
- Ruler
- Button
- Badge pin
- Electrical tape

1 Draw the shape of a cat's head on cardboard and cut it out. Cover the cardboard shape with three layers of papier-mâché and leave it in a warm place overnight or until the papier-mâché dries and hardens.

2 Paint both sides of the cat's head. When the paint is completely dry, varnish the front of the head with a water-based varnish or a mixture of white glue and water.

3 Cut two small triangles out of felt and glue them onto the cat's ears. Glue on gemstones for eyes. Cut pipe cleaners into three pieces, each approximately 1½ inches (4 centimeters) long, and glue them onto the face to make whiskers. Glue a button, for a nose, at the center of the pipe cleaners. Hold the button in place until the glue dries.

4 With black acrylic paint, paint eyelashes around the eyes and a mouth under the nose. Then paint an outline around the felt ears.

5 Glue a badge pin onto the back of the badge, toward the top of the cat's head. Let the glue dry, then secure the pin with electrical tape.

Speedy Car

This badge will impress everyone. The wheels actually move! You can paint passengers on the windows of the car, but why not cut out pictures of friends or family members from old photographs to glue onto the windows, instead?

YOU WILL NEED
- Pencil
- Cardboard
- Ruler
- Compass
- Scissors
- Acrylic paints
- Paintbrush
- White glue and glue brush
- Paper fasteners
- Badge pin
- Electrical tape

1 Draw the shape of a car on cardboard. The car should be about 4½ inches (11 cm) long by 3 inches (7.5 cm) high. Use a compass to draw two wheels, each about 1½ inches (4 cm) in diameter. Cut out all three shapes and paint them. Let the paint dry.

2 Cut out three 1-inch (2.5-cm) squares of cardboard and paint a picture of a person on each square. Let the paint dry, then glue the squares onto the top part of the car shape.

3 Ask an adult to poke holes, with the point of the compass — one hole in the center of each wheel and two in the bottom of the car. Push a paper fastener through the hole in each wheel and then through a hole in the car. Attach the wheels loosely, so they will spin around.

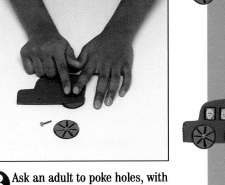

4 Glue a badge pin onto the back of the car. Let the glue dry, then secure the pin with electrical tape.

Feathery Chicken

This plucky chicken has felt feathers, and its bright yellow color really makes this clever badge stand out.

YOU WILL NEED
- Pencil
- Tracing paper
- Cardboard
- Scissors
- Acrylic paints
- Paintbrush
- Fabric marker or felt-tip pen
- Felt
- White glue and glue brush
- Pipe cleaners
- Ruler
- Badge pin
- Electrical tape

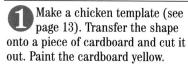

1 Make a chicken template (see page 13). Transfer the shape onto a piece of cardboard and cut it out. Paint the cardboard yellow.

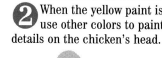

2 When the yellow paint is dry, use other colors to paint details on the chicken's head.

HANDY HINT
If you have scraps of felt in many different colors, cut some feathers out of each color and make a multicolored chicken.

3 Make a feather template (see page 13). Transfer the shape onto cardboard and cut it out. Use a fabric marker to draw around the shape on yellow felt. Draw lots of feathers this way and cut them out. Then, starting at the tail, glue the felt feathers onto the chicken.

4 Cut two pieces of pipe cleaner, each about 1 inch (2.5 cm) long, for the chicken's legs. Glue the legs onto the back of the chicken. Use a fabric marker to draw around the chicken on a piece of yellow felt. Cut out the felt shape and glue it onto the back of the chicken.

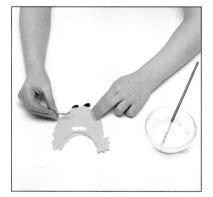

5 Glue a badge pin onto the felt backing, toward the top of the chicken. Let the glue dry, then secure the pin with electrical tape.

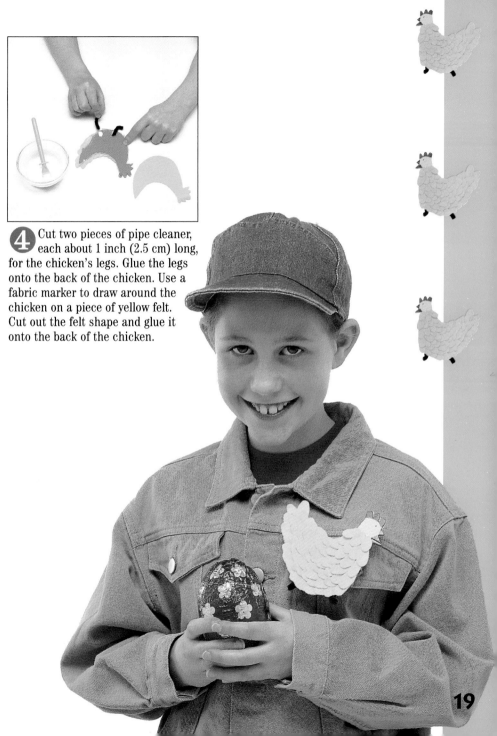

Magic Chest

Store tiny treasures in this magic chest and keep them close to you at all times!

YOU WILL NEED

- Small matchbox
- Craft knife
- Ruler
- Masking tape
- Shiny paper
- White glue and glue brush
- Acrylic paint
- Paintbrush
- Compass
- Paper fastener
- Star stickers
- Gemstones
- Badge pin
- Electrical tape

1 Ask an adult to cut three sides of a door into the front cover of a small matchbox, using a craft knife and a ruler. Leave the fourth side of the door uncut. Cover the matchbox, including the cut edges of the door, with masking tape to make it sturdier.

2 Cover the matchbox, including the door, with shiny paper. Stick down the edges and ends of the paper with glue. Let the glue dry.

3 Paint the inside of the matchbox. Let the paint dry completely.

4 Ask an adult to poke a hole in the door of the matchbox, using the sharp point of a compass. Push a paper fastener through the hole to make a door knob. Decorate the front of the door with shiny star stickers.

5 Glue colorful gemstones around the edge of the matchbox to decorate the door frame.

6 Glue a badge pin onto the back of the matchbox. Let the glue dry, then secure the pin with electrical tape.

Little House

Make this miniature house badge for a friend or family member. To make the project even more challenging, you can design the badge to look like the house where the person who will be wearing it lives.

YOU WILL NEED

- Large matchbox
- Masking tape
- Pencil
- Cardboard
- Scissors
- Felt
- White glue and glue brush
- Acrylic paints
- Paintbrush
- Colored paper
- Fabric paint
- Badge pin
- Electrical tape

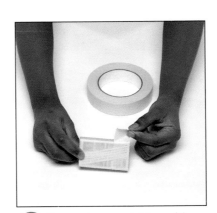

1 Cover a large matchbox with masking tape to make it sturdier. Draw the shape of a roof on a piece of cardboard and cut it out.

2 Cut a piece of felt to fit over the matchbox. Glue the felt onto the box. While the glue is drying, paint both sides of the roof. Let that paint dry before using black paint to add a design that looks like roof tile.

HANDY HINT

HANDY HINT

If you tape the matchbox carefully in step 1, so the inside part of the box will still slide in and out, you can hide small pieces of wrapped candy or some coins inside — for emergencies!

3 Cut out pieces of colored felt and colored paper to make the windows and door of the house. Glue them onto the front of the felt-covered matchbox. Finish decorating the house with fabric paint.

4 Glue the roof onto the top of the house and let the glue dry. Then glue a badge pin onto the back of the house near the roof. When the glue is dry, secure the pin with electrical tape.

Birthday Present

This easy-to-make badge is an ideal gift for a friend's birthday. You can attach it to a birthday card for a wonderful surprise!

YOU WILL NEED

- Scissors
- Colored cardboard
- Ruler
- Colored ribbons
- White glue and glue brush
- Pencil
- Colored paper
- Badge pin
- Electrical tape

1 Cut out a piece of colored cardboard that is 4 inches (10 cm) long and 3 inches (7.5 cm) wide. Cut two pieces of ribbon that are just long enough to overlap the length and the width of the cardboard. Glue the ribbon in place (as shown).

2 Draw the number of your friend's age on colored paper (shiny paper is best). Cut out the number and glue it over the ribbon on the present. Cut out small dots of colored paper and attach them to the ribbon with dabs of glue.

3 Tie a piece of brightly colored ribbon into a bow and glue the bow to the top of the present. Press firmly on the bow until the glue is completely dry.

4 Cut a piece of colored paper to cover the back of the present and glue it on. Glue a badge pin onto the back of the present, at the top. Let the glue dry, then secure the pin with electrical tape.

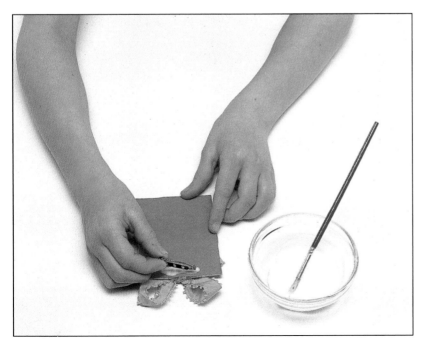

Crown Frame

When you are not wearing this badge, you can hang it on the wall or on your bedroom door.

YOU WILL NEED

- Pencil
- Cardboard
- Compass
- Scissors
- Newspaper
- White glue and glue brush
- Water
- Acrylic paint
- Paintbrush
- Fake fur
- Gemstones
- Ruler
- Badge pin
- Electrical tape

1 Draw the shape of a crown on cardboard and use a compass to draw a circle in the center of it. Cut out the crown and the circle. Put four layers of papier-mâché on the crown.

2 Let the papier-mâché dry overnight. Then paint both sides of the crown gold. Let the paint dry completely.

3 Cut a piece of fake fur the same size as the bottom of the crown. Glue the strip of fur along the bottom edge of the crown. Glue a gemstone to each point of the crown.

4 Cut out a cardboard square that is at least ¼ inch (½ cm) wider than the circle in the center of the crown. Brush glue along the edges of the square on only *three* sides, then press the square onto the back of the badge, covering the hole. The unglued side should be at the top. Paint the square gold. When the paint is dry, slide a photo into the frame.

5 Glue a badge pin onto the back of the crown, just under the points. Let the glue dry, then secure the pin with electrical tape.

HANDY HINT
When brushing glue along the edges of the cardboard square that covers the hole in the crown, be sure to leave enough space to slide a photo into the frame.

Felt Scotty Dog

Felt is a good fabric for this little dog. Besides being soft and fuzzy, felt is very easy to cut, and the edges do not fray. You can make other felt animal friends, too. Try a cat or a rabbit!

YOU WILL NEED

- Pencil
- Tracing paper
- Paper
- Scissors
- Straight pins
- Felt (two colors)
- Needle
- Thread
- Badge pin
- Ribbon

HANDY HINT

If you prefer, you can glue, rather than sew, the badge pin and bow to the fabric. You could also glue the two felt shapes together. Just remember to wait until the glue is completely dry before you try on the badge.

1 Make a dog template (see page 13). Transfer the pattern onto a piece of paper and cut it out. Pin the paper shape to a piece of felt and carefully cut around it. Cut out a second dog shape from another piece of felt in a different color.

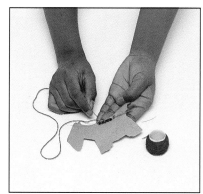

2 With a needle and thread, sew a badge pin onto the felt shape that you will use for the back of the dog. You might want to ask an adult to help you with the sewing.

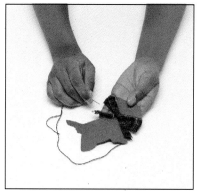

3 Tie a piece of ribbon into a bow, then sew the bow onto the neck of the felt shape that you will use for the front of the dog.

4 Pin together the front and back pieces of felt. Be sure the badge pin and the bow are on the outside. Use a running stitch around the entire edge of the dog to sew the pieces of felt together. Remember to remove the straight pins when you are finished sewing.

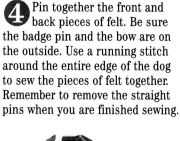

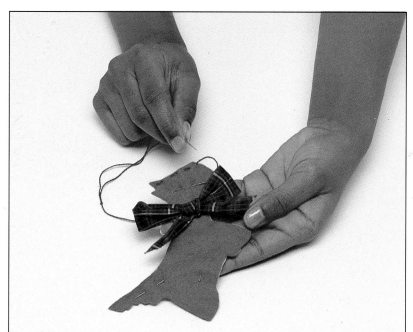

Clock Badge

You can control time with this portable clock — just twist the arms around to make it any time you want. This badge is perfect for anyone who likes to be on time!

YOU WILL NEED
- Compass
- Ruler
- Cardboard
- Scissors
- Acrylic paints
- Paintbrush
- Pencil
- Paper fastener
- White glue and glue brush
- Badge pin
- Electrical tape

1 Use a compass to draw a circle with a 6-inch (15-cm) diameter on a piece of cardboard. Cut out the circle.

2 Paint the cardboard a bright color. When the paint is completely dry, outline the edge of the circle with a different color paint.

3 To make the clock's face, use a pencil to draw in the numbers 1 through 12 around the edge of the circle. Then paint the numbers.

4 Draw two clock hands on a piece of cardboard and cut them out. Paint each of the clock hands a bright color.

5 Have an adult poke a hole in the end of each clock hand and in the center of the clock with the sharp point of the compass. Attach the hands to the face of the clock with a paper fastener.

6 Glue a badge pin onto the back of the clock, behind the number 12. Let the glue dry, then secure the pin with electrical tape.

Clay Fish

This fishy badge is very colorful — guaranteed to brighten up any outfit.

YOU WILL NEED
- Pencil
- Cardboard
- Scissors
- Rolling pin
- Self-hardening clay
- Ruler
- Modeling tool
- Acrylic paints
- Paintbrush
- White glue and glue brush
- Badge pin
- Electrical tape

1 Draw the shape of a fish on cardboard. Remember to add fins and a tail. Cut out the cardboard shape. Use a rolling pin to make a 4-inch (10-cm) square of clay that is ¼ inch (½ cm) thick. Place the cardboard shape on the clay and cut around it with a modeling tool.

2 With the sharp point of the modeling tool, carve features and patterns into the clay fish. Put the fish in a dry place and let it harden overnight.

3 Paint the front and back of the fish with a bright color. When the paint is completely dry, add some fun designs on the front of the fish in other bright colors. Always let each paint color dry completely before using a different color.

4 When the paint is completely dry, glue a badge pin onto the back of the fish, just under the top fin. Let the glue dry, then secure the pin with electrical tape.

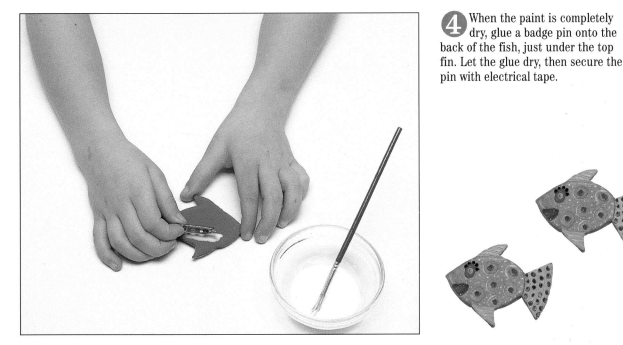

Glitzy Star

This dazzling badge is decorated with foil candy wrappers and shiny gemstones, sequins, and glitter. Wear the badge at parties and watch it sparkle!

YOU WILL NEED

- Pencil
- Cardboard
- Scissors
- Newspaper
- White glue and glue brush
- Water
- Foil candy wrappers
- Gemstones
- Sequins
- Glitter
- Badge pin
- Electrical tape

1. Draw the shape of a star on cardboard and cut it out. Cover the cardboard shape with three or four layers of papier-mâché. Let the papier-mâché dry overnight in a warm place.

2. Smooth out foil candy wrappers and glue them onto the front and back of the star.

3. Decorate the star by gluing on gemstones, sequins, and glitter. Let the glue dry completely.

4. Glue a badge pin onto the back of the star. Let the glue dry, then secure the pin with electrical tape.

Animals in a Field

This badge is full of surprises! Slide open the box to find miniature farm animals hidden inside. You can put any small objects into the box — or put special treasures inside for safekeeping.

YOU WILL NEED

- Scissors
- Grass paper
- Large matchbox
- White glue and glue brush
- Felt (two or more colors)
- Small plastic farm animals
- Badge pin
- Electrical tape

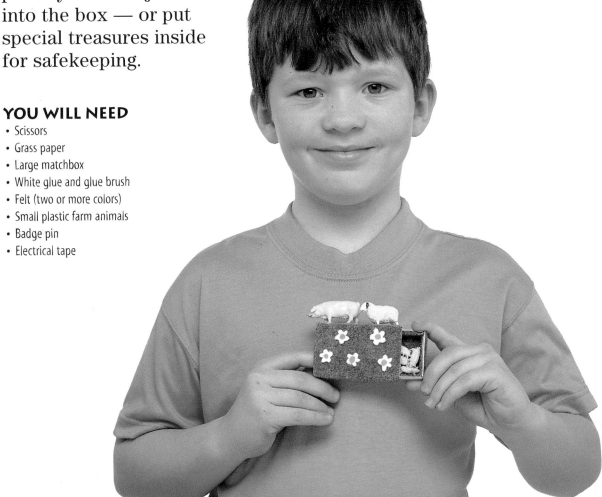

1 Cut grass paper to cover both the outside of a large matchbox and its inside drawer. Glue the grass paper down smoothly.

2 Cut out tiny felt flowers. Make the centers a different color then the petals. Glue the centers onto the petals and let the glue dry. Then glue the flowers to the grass paper on the cover of the matchbox.

3 Glue plastic farm animals along the top edge of the matchbox. Hold the animals in place until the glue dries. Put smaller farm animals inside the matchbox.

4 Glue a badge pin onto the back of the box. Let the glue dry, then secure the pin with electrical tape.

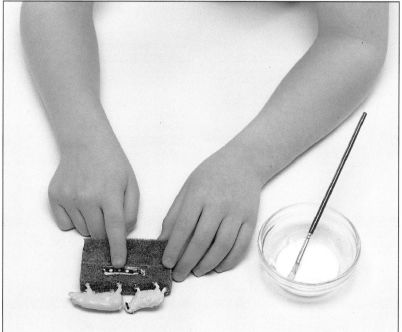

Fuzzy Orange

This bright orange badge is fun to make, and it will give your clothes a summery look. Have even more fun by making other fuzzy badges in a variety of fruit shapes and colors.

YOU WILL NEED
- Pencil
- Cardboard
- Scissors
- Acrylic paint
- Paintbrush
- White glue and glue brush
- Orange yarn
- Green felt
- Fabric paint
- Badge pin
- Electrical tape

1 Draw a circle on a piece of cardboard. The circle does not have to be perfectly round. Cut out the circle and paint it orange. Let the paint dry completely.

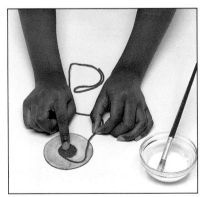

2 Coat one side of the circle with glue. Then, cut a long piece of orange yarn and, starting in the middle of the circle, coil the yarn around itself until the whole circle is covered with yarn.

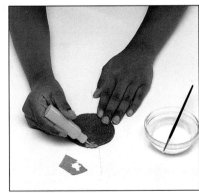

3 Cut a small, star-shaped leaf out of green felt. Glue the leaf to the top of the orange and dab a tiny blob of fabric paint on it where the stem of the orange would be.

4 When the glue is completely dry, turn the orange over and glue a badge pin onto the back. Let the glue dry, then secure the pin with electrical tape.

HANDY HINT
Without a badge pin attached, this piece of fuzzy fruit could also be a clever coaster for cold drinks on a hot day.

Salt Dough Badges

These badges are small and dainty, so you can make several and wear them together. They are great accessories for brightening up hats and bags, sweaters and sweatshirts.

YOU WILL NEED
- Rolling pin
- Salt dough
- Small cookie cutters
- Cookie sheet
- Sandpaper
- Acrylic paints
- Paintbrush
- White glue and glue brush
- Badge pins
- Electrical tape

1 Roll out salt dough on a flour-dusted surface and cut out small shapes with cookie cutters. Place the shapes on a greased cookie sheet and ask an adult to put the cookie sheet into the oven.

2 Bake the shapes for six hours at 250° Fahrenheit (120° Celsius). Let the baked shapes cool completely, then gently rub the surfaces with sandpaper to make them smooth.

3 Paint the front and back of each badge with a bright color. When the first coat of paint is completely dry, use other colors to add some designs.

4 Glue a badge pin onto the back of each shape. Let the glue dry, then secure each pin with electrical tape.

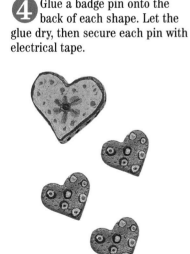

HANDY HINT

Save leftover dough in a plastic bag and store it in the refrigerator to use later.

41

Bow Tie

Wear this snazzy bow tie to a masquerade party, as part of a clown costume, or give the tie to a friend or to someone in your family as a fun clothing accessory.

1 Draw the shape of a bow tie on a piece of paper and cut it out. Pin the paper shape to a piece of felt and carefully cut around it. Make a second felt bow tie the same way.

2 Cut out ten or twelve felt dots in an assortment of colors. Glue the dots onto one of the felt bow ties. Let the glue dry.

3 Sew a badge pin to the center of the other felt bow tie. You might want to ask an adult to help you with the sewing.

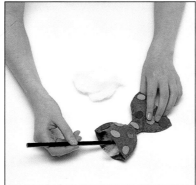

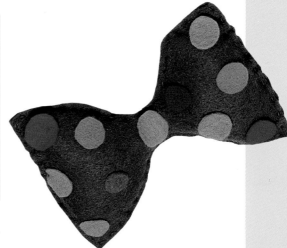

4 Pin the two felt bow ties together. Be sure the badge pin and the colored dots are on the outside. Use a running stitch around the edge of the bow tie to sew the pieces of felt together. Leave a small opening at one end for stuffing.

5 Remove the straight pins when you have finished sewing. Then fill the bow tie with stuffing material or scrunched-up tissue paper. Use a pencil, carefully, to push the stuffing into the corners of the tie. Now sew the opening closed.

Flower Power Badge

The flowers on this badge are not real. Use plastic or fabric flowers — so they will last forever. What a pretty gift for your mother or grandmother, or for a special friend!

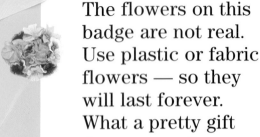

YOU WILL NEED

- Compass
- Cardboard
- Scissors
- Acrylic paint
- Paintbrush
- White glue and glue brush
- Artificial flowers
- Badge pin
- Electrical tape

1 Use a compass to draw two circles on a piece of cardboard. Cut out the circles and paint one of them a bright color. Let the paint dry.

2 Glue artificial flowers onto the painted circle. Use flowers in a variety of shapes and colors.

3 Cover the entire circle with flowers, holding each one firmly in place until the glue dries.

44

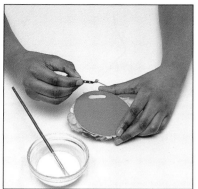

4 Glue the remaining cardboard circle onto the back of the badge and glue a badge pin onto the cardboard backing. Let the glue dry, then secure the pin with electrical tape.

HANDY HINT

If you make this badge with fabric flowers, try adding a light spray of cologne, or some other kind of fragrance, so the flowers will smell as lovely as they look.

Fluffy Snowman

This little snowman is wrapped in a cozy scarf to keep warm. If you do not have any cotton to make his fluffy snow, use scrunched-up white tissue paper instead.

YOU WILL NEED
- Pencil
- White cardboard
- Scissors
- Colored cardboard
- White glue and glue brush
- Cotton
- Fabric marker or felt-tip pen
- Felt (several colors)
- Badge pin
- Electrical tape

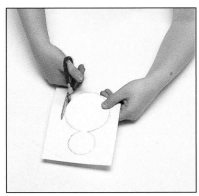

1 Draw the shape of a snowman on a piece of white cardboard and cut it out. Draw around this shape on a piece of colored cardboard. Cut out the colored cardboard shape and set it aside.

2 Coat one side of the white cardboard snowman with glue and press cotton onto the surface until the whole snowman is covered with cotton. Allow plenty of time for the glue to dry.

3 With a fabric marker, draw buttons and features for the snowman's face on pieces of felt and cut them out. Glue them in place on the cotton. Make a striped scarf by cutting two long pieces of felt and gluing on some narrow felt stripes and felt fringe in a contrasting color. Glue the scarf in place on the cotton.

4 Glue the colored cardboard shape onto the back of the snowman and glue a badge pin onto the back of the snowman's head. Let the glue dry, then secure the pin with electrical tape.

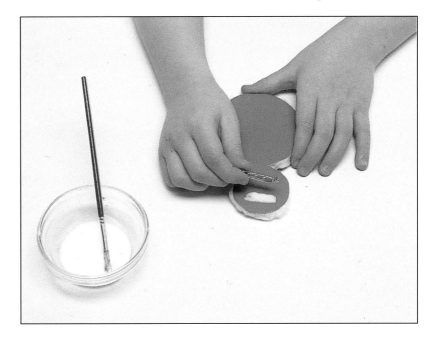

Happy Face

Brighten your day by wearing this cheerful face. Curly hair made out of pipe cleaners gives this badge a kooky look.

YOU WILL NEED

- Compass
- Ruler
- Cardboard
- Fabric marker or felt-tip pen
- Felt (several colors)
- Scissors
- Double-sided tape
- White glue and glue brush
- Fabric paints
- Pipe cleaners
- Pencil
- Colored paper
- Badge pin
- Electrical tape

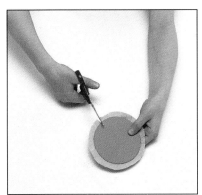

1 Use a compass to draw a circle, approximately 5 inches (12.5 cm) in diameter, on cardboard. With a fabric marker, draw another circle, ½ inch (1.3 cm) bigger than the cardboard circle, on a piece of felt. Cut out both circles and use double-sided tape to stick the cardboard circle in the middle of the felt circle. Make small cuts into the felt border surrounding the cardboard circle.

2 Fold over the pieces of felt between the cuts and glue them securely onto the back of the cardboard.

3 Cut out two felt ovals for eyes and glue them onto the felt circle. Use fabric paints to finish the eyes and to add a nose and a mouth.

4 Wind pipe cleaners around a pencil, to curl them, then glue them to the top of the head. Hold each one in place until the glue dries. On colored paper, draw a circle the same size as the face and cut it out.

5 Glue the paper circle onto the back of the face and glue a badge pin onto the paper backing, near the top of the head. Let the glue dry, then secure the pin with electrical tape.

Lollipop Badge

This lollipop badge looks so tasty you might want to eat it! It must **not**, however, be eaten. Although it is made with real candy, the candy is covered with varnish.

1 Use a compass to draw a circle 4 inches (10 cm) wide on cardboard. Cut out the circle.

2 Paint both sides of the circle a bright color and let the paint dry completely.

YOU WILL NEED

- Compass
- Ruler
- Cardboard
- Scissors
- Acrylic paint
- Paintbrush
- White glue and glue brush
- Small pieces of colorful hard candy
- Varnish
- Felt
- Ribbon
- Badge pin
- Electrical tape

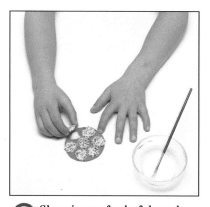

3 Glue pieces of colorful candy onto one side of the cardboard circle. When the glue is dry, coat the candy with varnish. Let the varnish dry completely.

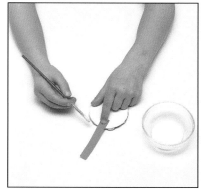

4 To make a stick for the lollipop, cut a strip of felt 1½ inches (3.8 cm) long and ½ inch (1.3 cm) wide. Glue one end of the felt strip to the back of the lollipop.

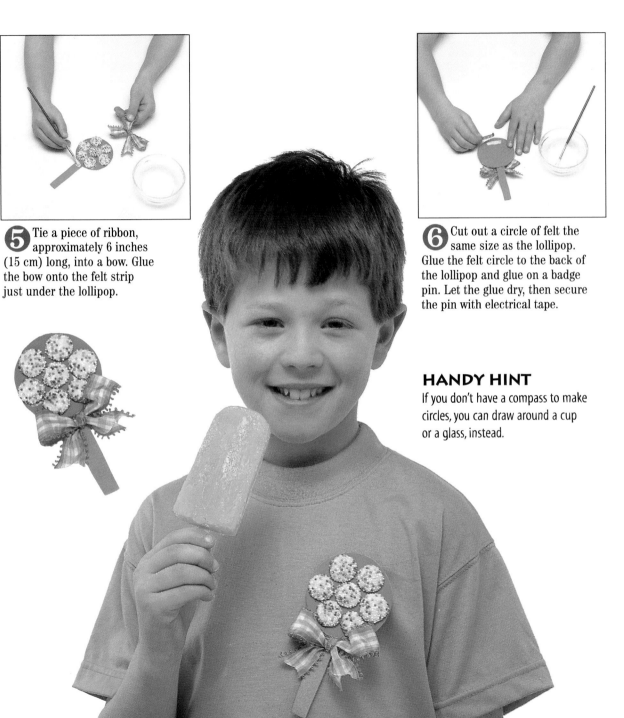

5 Tie a piece of ribbon, approximately 6 inches (15 cm) long, into a bow. Glue the bow onto the felt strip just under the lollipop.

6 Cut out a circle of felt the same size as the lollipop. Glue the felt circle to the back of the lollipop and glue on a badge pin. Let the glue dry, then secure the pin with electrical tape.

HANDY HINT

If you don't have a compass to make circles, you can draw around a cup or a glass, instead.

51

Butterfly

This beautiful salt dough butterfly is a perfect springtime accessory. It can really liven up a hat or a shirt, and salt dough is inexpensive and easy to make.

YOU WILL NEED
- Pencil
- Cardboard
- Scissors
- Rolling pin
- Salt dough
- Ruler
- Modeling tool
- Water
- Cookie sheet
- Sandpaper
- Acrylic paints
- Paintbrush
- White glue and glue brush
- Gemstones
- Badge pin
- Electrical tape

1 Draw the shape of a butterfly on a piece of cardboard and cut it out. Roll out salt dough on a flour-dusted surface until it is approximately ½ inch (1.3 cm) thick. Place the butterfly shape on the salt dough and carefully cut around it with a modeling tool.

2 Carve some decorations onto the butterfly with the modeling tool. You can decorate with small pieces of dough, too. Stick them onto the butterfly with water.

3 Put the butterfly on a cookie sheet and ask an adult to bake it for six hours at 250°F (120°C). Let the butterfly cool, then smooth out any roughness with sandpaper.

4 Paint patterns on the butterfly. When the paint is dry, glue a gemstone onto each wing and glue a badge pin onto the back of the butterfly. Let the glue dry, then secure the pin with electrical tape.

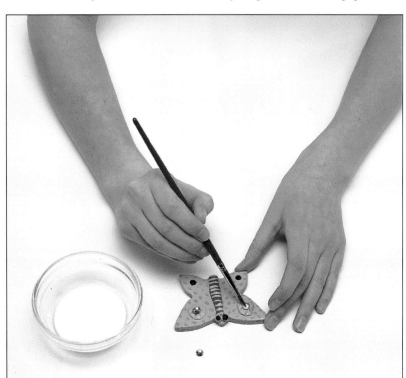

HANDY HINT

If you do not have a modeling tool, you can use the tip of a pencil or the edge of a ruler to cut and shape salt dough.

Paper Flower

This delicate paper flower makes a great finishing touch for any outfit, but be careful — it tears easily. Why not make several flowers in different colors, then join them to create a beautiful bouquet?

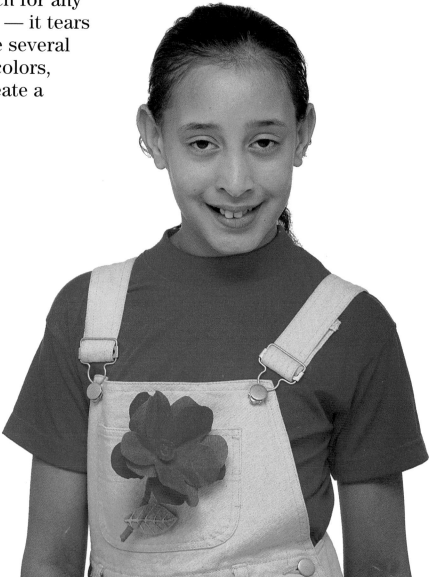

YOU WILL NEED

- Pencil
- Thin cardboard
- Scissors
- Crepe paper (three different colors)
- Compass
- Pipe cleaner
- Felt
- Ruler
- White glue and glue brush
- Fabric paint
- Needle
- Thread
- Badge pin

① Draw the shape of a flower on thin cardboard to use as a template. Cut out the shape, then draw around it on three pieces of crepe paper. Each piece of crepe paper should be a different color.

② Ask an adult to poke a hole in the center of each flower shape with the sharp point of a compass. Thread a pipe cleaner through the holes and coil the end of it to make the center of the flower. Scrunch up the crepe paper a little to make the flower look more natural.

③ Cut a strip of felt 8 inches (20 cm) long and 1 inch (2.5 cm) wide. Brush glue onto one side of the felt strip, then stick one end of the strip to the back of the flower and wrap the rest of it tightly around the pipe cleaner. Let the glue dry thoroughly.

④ Draw two identical leaf shapes on a piece of felt and cut them out. Glue one leaf to each side of the pipe-cleaner flower stem. Paint veins on the leaves with fabric paint.

⑤ Sew a badge pin at the top of the felt flower stem. Attaching the badge pin to the stem can be difficult. You might want to ask an adult to help with the sewing.

Birthday Badge

What could be a better present for a friend celebrating a birthday than a personalized birthday badge? This brightly decorated badge is made to show the age of the person wearing it.

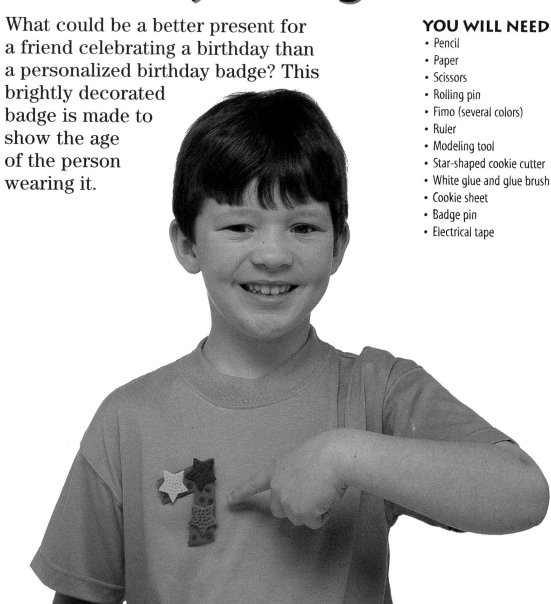

1 Draw the number for the appropriate age on a piece of paper and cut it out. Roll out a piece of Fimo until it is approximately ¼ inch (½ cm) thick. Place the paper number on the Fimo and cut around it with a modeling tool.

2 Roll out another piece of Fimo in a different color and cut out a star shape with a cookie cutter. Glue the star to the number. Repeat this step to make more stars in different colors.

3 Use the modeling tool to carve designs into the number, then carefully place the decorated number on a cookie sheet. Ask an adult to bake it for you, following the instructions on the Fimo package. Let the shape cool completely.

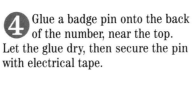

4 Glue a badge pin onto the back of the number, near the top. Let the glue dry, then secure the pin with electrical tape.

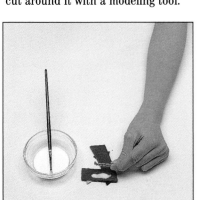

WARNING!

Fimo can be trickier to handle than clay or salt dough, and it requires special caution when baking to prevent dangerous fumes. Always read the instructions on the package and ask an adult to help you.

Button Heart

This badge makes a terrific Valentine's Day gift for a special someone.

YOU WILL NEED
- Pencil
- Cardboard
- Scissors
- Acrylic paint
- Paintbrush
- White glue and glue brush
- Buttons
- Ribbon
- Ruler
- Electrical tape
- Needle
- Thread
- Badge pin

1 Draw the shape of a heart on a piece of cardboard and cut it out. Paint the heart shape on both sides.

2 When the paint is completely dry, glue buttons onto one side of the heart.

3 Tie a piece of ribbon, approximately 10 inches (25 cm) long, into a bow. Glue the ends of the ribbon to the back of the heart so only the bow is showing at the top of the heart. Let the glue dry, then stick a piece of electrical tape over the ends of the ribbon.

4 Sew a badge pin to the back of the bow. You might want to ask an adult to help with the sewing.

HANDY HINT

When buying cardboard, ask for some that is thin enough to cut with scissors, yet stiff enough to stand up straight and hold its shape.

Dotty Dinosaur

This polka-dot dinosaur is made out of
Fimo. If you do not have any Fimo,
use another type of modeling
material, such as salt dough
or self-hardening clay.

YOU WILL NEED
- Pencil
- Cardboard
- Scissors
- Rolling pin
- Fimo (four colors)
- Ruler
- Modeling tool
- White glue and glue brush
- Cookie sheet
- Badge pin
- Electrical tape

① Draw the shape of a dinosaur on cardboard and cut it out. Roll out a piece of Fimo until it is approximately ¼ inch (½ cm) thick. Place the dinosaur shape on the Fimo and cut around it with a modeling tool.

② Roll out some Fimo in a different color and cut out four feet. Glue the feet onto the dinosaur. Cut some spikes out of Fimo in a third color and glue them along the top of the dinosaur's body.

③ Roll out more Fimo in a fourth color and cut out some small spots. Glue the spots onto the dinosaur's body, then carefully place the dinosaur on a cookie sheet. Ask an adult to bake it for you, following the instructions on the Fimo package. Let the shape cool completely.

④ Glue a badge pin onto the back of the dinosaur, near the top. Let the glue dry, then secure the pin with electrical tape.

HANDY HINT

More information about Fimo and other polymer modeling materials can be found at *www.polymerplanet.com*, "Your Online Resource for Polymer Clay." Click on "F.A.Q." for "Polyclay Frequently Asked Questions."

Glossary

accessory: an item or object that is not essential but adds to the overall look or usefulness of something else.

artificial: not natural; made by human beings to resemble, or look like, something natural.

coil: (v) to wind in a circle or spiral around and around a center point.

contrasting: showing differences that, usually, can be easily noticed when things are compared.

dabs: (n) light, quick touches, pats, or strokes.

dainty: pretty in a graceful and delicate way.

details: small, distinct parts of something bigger.

diameter: the straight line that runs through the center of a circle, from one edge to the other, determining the size (width) of the circle.

features: (n) specific parts of the face, such as the nose or the mouth; someone's or something's distinctive characteristics.

fray: to weaken, usually by pulling or rubbing, the threads or fibers of cloth, or other woven materials, until they become loose and unravel or separate.

knead: to mix ingredients by pressing or squeezing with the hands.

kooky: silly or goofy.

overlap: to spread or extend over something, covering at least part of it.

papier-mâché: scraps of newspaper coated with a mixture of white glue and water to form a pulplike substance that can be molded into strong, lightweight shapes.

personalized: made special or unique for a particular person.

running stitch: a way to sew by moving a needle and thread in and out of fabric in small, even stitches.

scrunched: crushed, crumpled, or squeezed together tightly into a wrinkled mass.

secure: (v) to attach or fasten firmly to hold something in a particular position.

snazzy: flashy and fancy.

template: a pattern used as a guide to make an identical shape or form on another piece of material.

transfer: to move an item or object from one place to another.

undiluted: not watered down or made thinner or weaker in any way; at full strength.

varnish: a clear, paintlike material that is spread on surfaces to give them a hard, shiny coating.

More Books To Read

Costume Crafts. Worldwide Crafts (series). Iain MacLeod-Brudenell (Gareth Stevens)

Creating with Salt Dough. Crafts for All Seasons (series). Anna Llimos and Laia Sadurni (Blackbirch Press)

Creative Clay Jewelry. Leslie Dierks (Lark Books)

Handmade Jewelry: Simple Steps to Creating Wearable Art. Carol Grape (North Light Books)

Hearts and Crafts. Sheri Brownrigg (Tricycle Press)

Jewellery Design Funstation. (Silver Dolphin)

Jewelry. World Crafts (series). Meryl Doney (Franklin Watts)

Make Pins: 16 Projects for Creating Beautiful Pins. Making Jewelry (series). Jo Moody (Rockport)

Making Jewelry. Step-By-Step (series). Sara Grisewood (Kingfisher Books)

You Can Do It!: Jewelry Making. You Can Do It! (series). Lana Gloria (Summit Publishing Group)

Videos

Jewelry from Recyclables. (Jomic, Inc.)

Kidvidz: Squiggles, Dots, and Lines. (Goldhil Home Media)

Let's Create Fun Jewelry for Boys and Girls. (Let's Create, Inc. – 1-888-CREATES – www.letscreate.com/jewelry.htm)

Web Sites

jewelrymaking.about.com/

www.michaels.com/projects/kp99146.html

Due to the dynamic nature of the Internet, some web sites stay current longer than others. To find additional web sites, use a reliable search engine with one or more of the following keywords: *art projects, clay, craft projects, Fimo, handicrafts, jewelry, papier-mâché, pins,* and *salt dough.*

Index